CALAMITY JANE

CALAMITY JANE

Her Life
and Her Legend

Illustrated with Photographs

DORIS FABER

Houghton Mifflin Company
Boston 1992

Library of Congress Cataloging-in-Publication Data

Faber, Doris, date.
  Calamity Jane : her life and her legend / Doris Faber.
    p.   cm.
  Includes bibliographical references.
  Summary: Examines the life of the Wild West heroine who was
transformed into a legendary figure in the public mind.
    ISBN 0-395-56396-8
    1. Calamity Jane, 1852–1903 — Juvenile literature.   2. Cowgirls —
West (U.S.) — Biography — Juvenile literature.   3. West (U.S.) —
Biography — Juvenile literature.   [1. Calamity Jane, 1852–1903.
2. Cowgirls.]   I. Title.
F594.C2F3   1992   91-40050
978'.02'092 — dc20   CIP
[B]   AC

Printed in the United States of America

HOR 10 9 8 7 6 5 4 3 2 1

Contents

CALAMITY JANE

Who Was She?

Almost everybody has heard of Calamity Jane.

What's more, the mere sound of her name gives the flavor of the old-time Wild West, so there can be no doubt about where and when she flourished.

But was she a real person or just a made-up character in adventure stories? The answer to this question is a little complicated.

Yes, there was a real woman nicknamed Calamity Jane, who loved to talk about having lived through many exciting adventures — but much of what she said could not really have happened the way she told it. There also was a writer who somehow got the idea of calling the imaginary heroine of some of his most popular tales Calamity Jane.

Then, around a hundred years ago, the actual person and the fictional heroine began merging in the public mind, creating the same kind of legendary figure as Johnny Appleseed, for instance.

Maybe this seems a bit confusing, and yet a similar process happened in the case of practically every famous hero from the great days of the American Wild West. Buffalo Bill, Wild Bill Hickok, Billy the Kid, all of them were transformed into legendary figures, celebrated less for what they actually did than for various imaginary exploits.

Many professors have tried to explain why the American West captured the imagination of people everywhere and inspired a whole

Calamity Jane in her early twenties. This is the earliest known picture of her, found around 1900 in an old Deadwood building that was being torn down. (Library of Congress)

"Westward Ho, or The Spirit of the Frontier," by John Gast in 1872, shows the prevailing idea that women's role was to inspire men — not to seek adventure of their own. (Library of Congress)

new set of legends — at least roughly along the lines of Europe's legends about medieval knights in armor. According to some of these theories, reading about the West's spectacular open spaces offered even the unadventurous a magical escape from the pressures of more settled areas. Others point out that the high drama involved in venturing into the wilderness provided marvelous opportunities for spinning tall tales with larger-than-life heroes and villains.

Books have been written about this topic, but here we can only note that legends require fitting heroines as well as heroes. And now it is time to start taking a closer look at the leading heroine of the legendary Wild West by making the acquaintance of a lively farm girl who could not stand following any rules about proper female behavior.

Pony Girl

Her real name was Martha Jane Cannary. As she put it herself, "Born in Princeton, Missouri, May 1st, 1852." To be more precise, her birthplace was a cabin on a backwoods farm near that small town in the northern part of the nation's twenty-fourth state.

Her parents had come out there from Ohio a few years earlier. But hardly anything else can be said about them — they were not the sort of pioneers who saved trunkfuls of old letters or other papers in case anybody might want to compile their family history.

Perhaps Robert and Charlotte Cannary had a lot of hard luck. Or maybe they were just too frail, or too easygoing, to tame land that as recently as the 1820s had been part of a trackless forest. Whatever the reason, they failed at farming and probably would have been completely forgotten if the eldest of their six children had not become famous.

She became famous as Calamity Jane, who did a lot of cheerful bragging throughout her lifetime. Right at the outset, though, we have to face a disappointing fact: a good many of the adventures she claimed to have braved never actually happened. Alas, her tales about serving as a scout for General Custer or single-handedly saving the Deadwood stage from bandits were not actually true.

Still, her daredevil talk of boldly competing with the likes of

Buffalo Bill certainly helped to bring about the birth of the legendary figure named after her. And by now the legend of Calamity Jane has become a genuine part of our national heritage — of far more significance than the true story of the life of Martha Jane Cannary. Even so, that lively, excitement-loving Missouri farm girl deserves our attention because she at least wished she could be somebody special.

In her youth, she was known as Marthy.

Marthy probably had little or no schooling. Since she grew up in an isolated area, with five younger brothers and sisters to be looked after, chances are that nobody cared if she never learned to read or write. Clearly, though, there was a spark within her that soon made her stand out.

Years later, when she had attracted so much notice that somebody helped her issue a booklet about her memories, she devoted only a few sentences to her beginnings. What she stressed most was her special fondness for horses. As she told it: "I began to ride at an early age and continued to do so until I became an expert rider, being able to ride the most vicious and stubborn of horses, in fact the greater portion of my life in early times was spent in this manner."

When Marthy was thirteen, her parents made a decision that opened up all sorts of thrilling possibilities for her. The Civil War was being fought in the more settled part of the country and, even in remote Missouri, gangs of raiders favoring one side or the other galloped around causing trouble for their enemies. Yet this turmoil does not seem to have had anything to do with the Cannary plan to pick up and move farther westward.

More likely, Marthy's parents were just worn out by their hardscrabble farming and tired of being looked down on by their neighbors. Not involved in any of the burning issues of the day, they did not even have any definite goal as they packed their few belongings into a wagon. One fine morning in the spring of 1865, they set forth.

Pioneers' covered wagons winding downhill to cross a river along the Overland Trail.
(Smithsonian Institution)

They went first to the Missouri town named Independence. On a big bend of the Missouri River, Independence was the jumping-off point for wagon trains taking the famous Overland Trail toward Oregon. Although pioneers' wheels had already worn deep ruts marking this route northwest through the Great Plains and the Rocky Mountains, attacks by Indians remained a constant threat. So a family traveling by itself would aim to join up with others, hoping to have safety in numbers.

Most families leaving Independence had large wagons covered with a double thickness of canvas, loaded with such a weight of possessions and provisions that it took four to six yoke of oxen to pull them. No

A typical pioneer family, and the wagon in which they lived and traveled for many months. (National Archives)

doubt the Cannary rig was on the light side. But it was Marthy's own behavior throughout her westward trek that set her apart.

Today it is almost impossible to realize how strong — and how silly — many of the prevailing ideas about the proper behavior of females were back in Marthy's era. For instance, another girl who went West with her family wrote an account of her trip in which she recalled: "While traveling, mother was particular about Louvina and me wearing sunbonnets and long mitts in order to protect our complexions, hair and hands. Much of the time I should like to have gone without that long bonnet poking out over my face, but . . . I stuck to my bonnet, finally growing used to it. . . . When riding, I always rode {sidesaddle} with my full skirt pulled well down over my ankles. If we had ridden astride . . . people would have thought we were not lady-like. Mother was always reminding Louvina and me to be ladies."

Marthy, on the other hand, brashly wore borrowed trousers, and "the greater part of my time was spent in hunting along with the men of the party, in fact I was at all times with the men when there was excitement and adventures to be had." She went on: "We had many dangers to encounter in the way of streams swelling on account of heavy rains . . . on more than one occasion {I} mounted my pony and swam across the stream several times merely to amuse myself and had many narrow escapes from having both myself and pony washed away to certain death."

Five months after leaving Missouri, Marthy and her family veered off from the rest of their party to try their luck in a rough Montana mining camp grandly named Virginia City. Only thirteen, she already could cuss as fiercely as any man and she had even learned to like the taste of whiskey.

All Over the Map

About ten years earlier, in 1855, several men who had been disappointed in their quest for gold in California were on their way eastward when one of them got sick. While he was recuperating, his buddies did some prospecting along the bed of a Montana creek and found a few grains of yellow dust. Then a band of Blackfoot Indians discouraged further search.

The whites returned in 1863, though, and panned enough bright dust to start a fair-sized gold rush. By the time Marthy and her family arrived in Virginia City two years later, it was the main settlement of a mining area stretching twenty miles along the rocky creek that had been named Alder Gulch. About fifteen thousand newcomers were housed in shacks or tents or just sleeping under the stars, wrapped in blankets.

It was autumn when the Cannary wagon parked among them and, though the towering pines on the mountain slopes remained deep green, the creek-side alder leaves had begun to wither. Did the first hard frost convince Marthy's parents that they were not destined to get rich quickly here after all? Or did they stay in the vicinity, with just a makeshift shelter, throughout the harsh Montana winter?

Nobody can say; Marthy's account merely notes that her mother died in another part of Montana the following year, and her father

At a gold miners' camp in the western mountains. (National Archives)

died a year later hundreds of miles southward in Utah. Not a word does she add about what happened to her two brothers and three sisters.

As for Marthy herself, around the age of sixteen she began making her own way all over the map out West, behaving so fearlessly and outrageously that she was bound to be noticed.

To start with, she tried to earn her keep by working at proper female occupations like cooking or washing clothes. Such tame activity did not suit her. Aiming to get around the many rules restricting girls and women, she soon gave up wearing skirts and pretended to be a boy so she could get hired for more exciting jobs.

Although Marthy must have been slender and boyish-looking then, no pictures of her dating back to her teens have turned up. No reliable descriptions of her have turned up either. Later on, some old-timers would insist that her hair had been the rich reddish-brown of a shiny chestnut, whereas others remembered it as jet black, like an Indian's.

At any rate, toward the end of the 1860s when the tracks for the nation's first transcontinental railroad were being laid, one of the work crews out in Wyoming included a young fellow whose true identity did not remain secret for long.

Because the work party was advancing through a region sacred to Sioux and Cheyennes, an armed guard of soldiers protected it. Marthy had already discovered that she enjoyed nothing better than flirting with soldiers. When sharp-eyed soldiers invited this "boy" to come swimming after hours in a stream near their camp, she recklessly tore off her clothes and joined in the splashing. As a result, the next day she was ordered to depart eastward with a train of supply wagons.

A work gang laying tracks for the nation's first transcontinental railroad.
(Smithsonian Institution)

Workers' campsite during construction of the first railroad to the Pacific.
(National Archives)

"Such acres of wagons!" exclaimed Horace Greeley, the editor of the New York *Tribune,* when he visited the main depot of the Kansas company that supplied the West before railroads took over. "Such herds of oxen! Such regiments of drivers."

Marthy joined them. Off and on for years, she worked as a bull-whacker — driving what Westerners called bull teams. These were pairs of oxen yoked to strings of wagons that had been loaded with all sorts of goods, from railroad ties to baskets of potatoes. Her pay ranged between fifty and seventy-five dollars a month, plus all the bread, bacon, and coffee she could consume, which was a good deal in those days and much better than she could have done by washing clothes. In addition, the job provided plenty of challenge.

Up and down steep trails, through mud or across rocky streambeds, bullwhackers had to walk beside their animals and keep them moving in the right direction, day after day. One of the main requirements for this line of work was an ability to snap a twenty-foot whip with sufficient skill to flip a fly off the ear of an ox way in the front, even if you seemed to be just sauntering along and admiring the scenery. A talent for cursing ferociously to keep your animals on the move was almost as important.

While Marthy became an expert in both of these departments, she also acquired an increasing thirst for raw, frontier whiskey. Nobody who encountered her believed more than briefly that she was a boy, so a problem arose: What could you call a female who somehow got away with defying so many rules?

A bullwhacker and his train of supply wagons on their way to the Black Hills. (*Library of Congress*)

Ox teams resting in the main street of a Dakota town. (Library of Congress)

At least half a dozen stories have been told about the origin of the name Calamity Jane. According to the one she herself told, once when she was riding her horse out near Goose Creek in Wyoming she came upon some soldiers trying to put down an Indian uprising. Right before her eyes, a captain named Egan got shot and "I lifted him onto my horse in front of me and succeeded in getting him safely to the fort. Captain Egan on recovering laughingly said, 'I name you Calamity Jane, the heroine of the plains.'"

But Captain Egan denied that anything of the sort had ever taken place. His denial is not surprising, for Calamity Jane grew increasingly careless about telling the truth as her career advanced. Still, this weakness of hers was common in the wide open spaces — a talent for telling tall tales entertainingly was highly valued — and the stories other people told about how she got her nickname shared a similar improbability.

Western history experts suggest that the most likely explanation is that, in the slang of the era, any female might be referred to as a jane.

Therefore, a female who kept turning up where shootings or other dreadful events were occurring could easily strike an observer as a regular calamity jane. Even minor characters on the Western scene received catchy nicknames like Pinto Pete or Poker Alice, but no other woman got a tag that caught on the way Martha Jane Cannary's did.

No matter how it started, she relished her new title hugely. Whenever she arrived in a town where nobody knew her, if she had some money in her pocket she would stride through the swinging doors of the first barroom she came to, shouting: "I'm Calamity Jane and the drinks are on me!"

Scout for General Custer

They were called the Black Hills because their slopes were thickly covered with a kind of pine that, when seen from a distance, looked inky dark. Their valleys had such terrible tangles of underbrush as to make them nearly impassable, and the entire area was noted for the frequency and ferocity of its thunderstorms.

Still, soon after Calamity turned twenty, rumors began to circulate that there was a lot of gold in those Black Hills of Dakota, just waiting to be discovered. The rumors traveled all the way to Washington and, during the spring of 1875, the government sent a party of geologists to find out if the tales had any solid basis. Since much of the region belonged to a Sioux reservation, soldiers from the nearest U.S. fort were assigned to protect the scientists.

Calamity Jane traveled with the expedition, too. Not that she thought of taking up prospecting herself — she always enjoyed roaming more than staying put in any particular place. But even though she was mainly seeking the excitement of exploring in a new direction when she went along as one of the drivers of supply wagons, she soon developed another ambition.

It was to be an army scout. Out in the western territories where detachments of soldiers occupied isolated forts flying the American flag, officers and men with regular military training often found

Mounted soldiers, commanded by General Custer, and their supply wagons, crossing the plains of the Dakota Territory. (National Archives)

themselves at a loss. They needed someone who could show them the best route through a seemingly impenetrable canyon or warn them of dangerous rapids ahead or reliably deliver messages to their headquarters. In short, they needed a corps of fearless aides experienced in the ways of the West.

The most famous army scout of the era was William F. Cody, better known as Buffalo Bill owing to his skill as a buffalo hunter. Yet the majority of the scouts in Dakota during the 1870s were Pawnee or other Indians who hated the Sioux more than they feared white interlopers.

Did Calamity Jane achieve her goal of joining their ranks?

According to her own story, she not only carried out numerous scouting missions, she even scouted for the renowned General Custer, one of the nation's most popular heroes.

George Armstrong Custer had been the youngest general in the Union army during the Civil War, only twenty-four when his dashing leadership of a cavalry brigade brought his promotion. He rode to increasing fame when his volunteers on horseback played an important part in beating back Confederate forces at Gettysburg and in several other battles. The fact that he was very handsome and loved to pose

An army camp near Pine Ridge, South Dakota, in 1891. (Library of Congress)

General Custer. (Library of Congress)

No actual picture of Custer's Last Stand exists, but thousands of copies of this imagined scene were displayed around the country. (Smithsonian Institution)

for pictures also helped to advance his career.

But, in an army court, other officers accused Custer of having poor judgment, as well as too much fondness for personal glory. Even so, eleven years after the Civil War had ended he was commanding his old regiment of mounted troopers in the Dakota Territory. Early in the spring of 1876, when a report from the geologists confirmed the rumors about gold in the Black Hills, Custer was ordered there to guard a sudden rush of would-be miners.

Only a few months later, the general and over two hundred of his men attacked a large Sioux encampment on the banks of the Little Bighorn River. On June 25, 1876, Custer and everybody with him died in the horrendous slaughter that has gone down in history as Custer's Last Stand.

Miners washing and panning gold. (*Library of Congress*)

Calamity Jane would always insist that if not for a lucky mishap, she would have died there, too. In her own words: "During this march [toward the Little Bighorn] I swam the Platte River at Fort Fetterman as I was the bearer of important despatches. I had a ninety mile ride to make. Being cold and wet I contracted a severe illness and was sent back to Fort Fetterman where I [lay] in the hospital for fourteen days."

If she had not caught pneumonia, Calamity explained, she would have rejoined her comrades right before the fatal attack, and then surely she would have been killed with them. However, so many details of her story raise questions about their truthfulness — for instance, she mentioned meeting Custer at a fort not even built until after his death — that most experts scoff at Calamity's story of her career as a scout.

Possibly, though, she did carry at least a few messages or otherwise assist Custer. Officials in Washington never recorded any payment to

Soldiers camping at Whitewood in the Dakota Territory in 1876, using tents improvised from wagon frames. (Archives)

Along the Platte River near one of the army forts where Calamity Jane said she had been based during her scouting days. (Smithsonian Institution)

a scout named Cannary, but maybe she was using another name or maybe she was paid informally without any evidence being sent to higher authorities. For she really was in the Black Hills during this period — brief references to Calamity Jane have turned up in too many diaries and old newspapers to doubt her presence at the start of the rowdy gold rush centering around the new settlement of Deadwood.

However, most of the references mention her only as part of a group of women scorned by the high-minded. Women who were willing to do laundry for soldiers and otherwise keep them company often followed army units wherever they went; they were called camp followers. Without any question, Calamity Jane fitted into this category.

Scout or not, she always liked to drink with men and she also loved quite a number of men. Yet she differed from the "hurdy-gurdy girls" who worked in Western dance halls, earning their living by loving any man willing to pay them. Instead, Calamity married one man after another, at least unofficially.

Calamity's Husbands

Over the years, Calamity claimed to have married about a dozen different men. At various times, in various places, she lived with soldiers, ranchers, and miners she called her husbands. But most of their names have long since been forgotten. The only one that history remembers is the celebrated frontier marshal Wild Bill Hickok.

Like so much else in Calamity's life, her romance with Wild Bill probably did not happen exactly the way she herself recalled it. Whether it happened at all can be seriously doubted. Nevertheless, her story combines such a satisfying mixture of dramatic Wild West ingredients that even nowadays it continues to stir the emotions of thousands of tourists who visit Deadwood, South Dakota, where the two of them are buried together.

According to Calamity, as soon as she had recovered from the case of pneumonia that had marvelously saved her from death at Little Bighorn, she rode off to a Wyoming fort and there encountered the famous Wild Bill for the first time. Baptized James Butler Hickok back in Illinois thirty-nine years earlier, he had earned his nickname by his speed and accuracy in gun battles with outlaws after he became a U.S. marshal in the West. Already a living legend, he had just returned from a tour of the East in a stage show costarring Buffalo Bill.

Deadwood in 1876. (Library of Congress)

Wild Bill certainly looked like a Western hero, with an enormous straw-colored mustache and eyes of steel. The elegant fringed outfits that he wore set him further apart from the ordinary run of dusty frontiersmen. Undoubtedly, Calamity was deeply impressed by him.

Was he similarly impressed by a brash, trouser-wearing, twenty-four-year-old female who aimed to ride and shoot as fast as any male? Although nobody else noticed any sign of interest on his part, Calamity reported about twenty years later that the two of them had ridden off together toward the new Dakota boom town in Deadwood Gulch — and, along the trail, had met a lone man on horseback who turned out to be a preacher.

At Wild Bill's request, she would say, the preacher spoke the words that legally married them. He even signed his name to a certificate he found in his knapsack. When this document eventually turned up, suspicious individuals discovered no trace of the preacher whose name was written on it. Furthermore, there was plenty of evidence that in 1876 Wild Bill already had a wife — the part owner of a circus back East.

Yet Calamity claimed that she did not suspect this herself, despite Wild Bill's telling her, when they reached Deadwood, that he wanted to keep their marriage secret for a while. Happily, she started an exciting new job as a pony express rider, carrying U.S. mail between Deadwood and a settlement called Custer, a distance of fifty miles over one of the roughest trails in the Black Hills country.

For the next month or so, her story continued, she made a round trip every two days without any trouble. Even though the route was considered extremely dangerous because there could be large amounts of gold in the mail sacks leaving Deadwood, no bandits bothered her, owing to her reputation as an unbeatable rider and a crack shot.

Then, on the second of August, when Calamity returned to Deadwood, she heard stunning news. One of the most spectacular crimes ever committed in the West had just taken her husband's life. As Wild Bill had sat playing poker in the local establishment called the Number 10 Saloon — carefully facing its front door, and unaware of any other entrance — a lowdown character named Jack McCall had

After the original monument at Wild Bill Hickok's grave was torn down, a friend put up this elaborate pillar. (Library of Congress)

The Deadwood stage following another coach across a wooden bridge near the town.
(Library of Congress)

come striding through a small rear door and aimed right at his head.

Deadwood buried Wild Bill in a coffin richly trimmed with silver, and his closest friend, Colorado Charlie Utter, put up an elaborate gravestone on which was carved: "Pard we will meet again in the Happy Hunting Ground to part no more."

As for Calamity, she tried her best to rise above her grief. Only a few months later, she said, she accomplished one of her greatest feats, single-handedly saving the Cheyenne-to-Deadwood stage after its driver had been shot. Somehow jumping aboard to take the reins dropped by the dead driver, she got the horses under control and drove

Street scene in old Deadwood. (Centennial Archives, Deadwood Public Library)

the remaining twelve miles without any further difficulty, much to the relief of the coach's six passengers.

Of course, most of this might be just what Calamity wished to believe. According to the best available evidence, what really happened is that she sank deeper and deeper into the sad life of a helpless alcoholic. Still, between her drinking binges, her generous willingness to assist anybody who seemed to need help made the people who knew her agree that Calam was someone you had to like after all.

Besides taking care of neglected children from time to time, she tended people suffering from typhoid or some other fever. Indeed, her skill as a nurse caused more than a few to call her the frontier's Florence Nightingale, comparing her to the English lady whose organizing of hospitals during the Crimean War of the 1850s had for all practical purposes founded the nursing profession.

Much to the distress of moralists, however, every year or two Calamity showed up in one town or another with a new husband. Dorsett and Somers, Hunt, Steers, and Dalton, these were only some of the last names she temporarily adopted. But it was a man she never met who in 1877 began making Calamity Jane's own name famous.

The Contributions
of Ned Wheeler

Edward Lytton Wheeler — Ned for short — was born in upstate
New York in 1854, making him two years younger than Martha Jane
Cannary. While he was still a baby, his family moved to the western
Pennsylvania town of Titusville, where the first oil well in the United
States had just been drilled. Titusville, as far as anybody has been able
to discover, was the farthest west he ever went.

But Ned Wheeler, whose parents ran a boarding house, grew into
the sort of bookish boy who started writing stories during his school
days. By the time he turned twenty, his tales were appearing in the
Philadelphia "story papers" that came out every week filled with lively
if not very literary adventure yarns. Since real newspapers printed
accounts of Indian fights or other high drama in the territories beyond
the Missouri River, Ned borrowed a few details — and then made up
a lot of complications involving villains who always got their come-
uppance at the last minute from amazingly lucky heroes.

Some of Wheeler's earliest efforts had titles like "Hurricane Nell,
the Girl Dead-Shot" or "Wild Edna, the Girl Bandit," so he must
have been fascinated by the idea of having a daring female as his

In the old days, packages of chewing tobacco contained cards showing Wild West scenes. This one, "Painting the Town Red," pictures the sort of rowdy celebrating Calamity Jane enjoyed. (Smithsonian Institution)

leading character. Still, it was not until he started selling his work to a pair of extremely shrewd publishers in New York that he began calling his heroine Calamity Jane.

The team of Beadle and Adams is generally credited with inventing one of the most popular types of reading material in American history — famous as the dime novel, even though sometimes the price was only a nickel. By 1877, when Wheeler began writing for them, they were issuing every week about twenty different booklets the size of a thin modern magazine. Despite having just one drawing, on their cover, they attracted millions of readers for several decades, until they were supplanted by more up-to-date publications.

The front page of the first in the long series of Deadwood Dick dime novels, featuring Calamity Jane. (Library of Congress)

Maybe either Beadle or Adams had somehow come across the name of an outrageous Western female known as Calamity Jane. Or maybe Ned Wheeler had found some clue and then used his fertile imagination to expand on it. Yet it is also possible that he dreamed up the name all on his own — very little can be positively said about the career of this nearly forgotten author, except that the printed heading of his writing paper read: "Studio of Edward L. Wheeler, Sensational Novelist."

While Wheeler was only one of many Beadle and Adams writers who turned out fresh stories filling fourteen closely printed pages almost every week, his series featuring Calamity Jane became especially popular. However, a fact that may distress some of her admirers must now be mentioned. Although Calamity's role in defeating villains was often crucial in the dozens of dime novels across whose pages she galloped fearlessly, the title of the series featuring her came from the name of its totally imaginary hero, Deadwood Dick.

Sometimes Calamity received the status of a costar, for instance in "Deadwood Dick on Deck; or, Calamity Jane, the Heroine of Whoop-Up." Perhaps Beadle and Adams were convinced that boys and men would not want to read an adventure tale if it lacked a leading man. Nevertheless, Calamity repeatedly saved Dick from being hanged or hacked to pieces or blown up in mine explosions, while she herself managed to stay alive without any such assistance from him.

"She's a brick, Sandy," one old-timer told another as they heard her singing a wild but sweet song while she rode along the trail into Deadwood on the first page of one of her adventures, "and just let et pop right inter yer noodle that she ain't no fool. She's a dare-devil, Sandy . . . the most reckless buckaroo in these Hills."

And here she is, rushing to stave off the destruction of the Whoop-Up mine: "She dashed madly down through the gulch, standing erect upon the back of her unsaddled horse and the animal running at the

Front page of a dime novel featuring Calamity Jane. (*Denver Public Library, Western History Department*)

top of its speed . . . still the dare-devil retained her position as if glued to the animal's back, her hair flowing wildly from beneath the brim of her slouch hat, her eyes dancing occasionally with excitement, every now and then her lips giving vent to a ringing whoop, which was creditable imitation if not in volume and force to that of a full-blown Comanche warrior."

Dressed in buckskin trousers adorned with fancifully beaded leggings, and a velvet vest set off by a rich gold chain strung across its front, she looked "regally beautiful," according to Sandy. Racing along, she seemed to catch with delight "long breaths of the perfume of flowers which met her nostrils at every onward leap of her horse." Then, "piercing the gloom of the night with her dark, lovely eyes, searchingly, lest she should be surprised, she lit a cigar at full motion — dashing on, on, this strange girl of the Hills went, on her flying steed."

Any effort to summarize even one of the adventures that Ned Wheeler gave Calamity is doomed to failure because their plots have so many twists and turns, as well as incredible coincidences and mysterious disguises. Still, they are no more fantastic than some of today's comic strips. And they certainly had a similar impact.

A couple of generations of boys, and no doubt many girls, too, grew up reading Calamity stories when they were supposed to be studying algebra. As a result, her name entered the English language — any independent-minded female who disregarded rules about proper ladylike behavior could find herself being referred to as another Calamity Jane.

Her Own Story

Of course, the image of Calamity Jane that was spread by dime novels had little or no resemblance to the real life of Martha Jane Cannary. So an odd sort of difference developed during the 1870s, 1880s, and 1890s. Among those who merely read about her, she inspired increasing admiration, and even awe, while those who actually knew her felt increasing pity, or even disgust.

For as the years passed the real Calamity went sadly downhill — in one town after another, she drank so much that she collapsed like a large pile of rags. Repeatedly, she was clapped into jail and kept behind bars for a few days until she sobered up.

In these same years, the Wild West was tamed and growing numbers of tourists arrived every summer from the East. Thrilling tales about the wide-open spaces had stirred readers as far away as Europe, so many well-off foreign travelers made the trip, too. Besides marveling at the West's spectacular scenery, the visitors asked a lot of questions about the colorful characters they had read about.

When they asked about Calamity Jane, the answer often was a baffled stare. It seemed that the farther away people came from, the more famous her name had become. But in former mining camps that were turning into respectable towns, prouder of their new churches than of their old saloons, the idea that such a low type of female could

Calamity Jane dressed up for a visit to the grave of Wild Bill Hickok.
(Library of Congress)

be looked upon as a heroine struck many of the high-minded as ridiculous.

Nevertheless, Calamity still had plenty of long-time friends who loved to hear her tell of her adventures and who praised her for her many kindnesses during the intervals between her drinking, especially her care of sick people. "Sure, she's awfully goodhearted," they said.

What's more, some new acquaintances tried to get her back on the right track. Around the middle of the 1890s, when Calamity looked as old as the hills even though she was only in her forties, a woman who wrote for newspapers back East convinced her that she ought to cash in on her fame as a pony express rider by appearing in shows, the way various other early Western figures had. Why, Buffalo Bill had been making a fortune by taking his own Wild West show all over America and Europe.

So, with the help of her friends, Calamity got herself outfitted in a fancy fringed suit and shiny leather boots. The best job she could get, though, was with a small company that put on performances in various Midwestern cities. Perhaps her reputation as a drinker kept the bigger firms from hiring her. But here is how Kohl & Middleton advertised her first appearance in Minneapolis:

Week Beginning Monday, Jan. 20

CALAMITY JANE!

The Famous Woman Scout of the Wild West!
Heroine of a Thousand Thrilling Adventures!
The Terror of Evildoers in the Black Hills!
The Comrade of Buffalo Bill and Wild Bill!
See This Famous Woman and Hear Her Graphic Description of Her
Daring Exploits!
A HOST OF OTHER ATTRACTIONS
That's all — ONE DIME! — That's all.

However, Calamity Jane quickly found that she hated being stared at by a parcel of strangers. She got tongue-tied when she tried to tell her stories from a stage, instead of just standing around companionably with a batch of buddies. To keep up her courage, she ignored her promise about drinking — and was soon fired.

Buffalo Bill. (Library of Congress)

A couple of years later, she got one more chance. She was back in Deadwood then, where she had had her happiest times, and someone there helped her put her own story down, in a booklet entitled *Life and Adventures of Calamity Jane by Herself.* A local printer provided her with a big stack of copies. The plan was that she herself would sell them in Buffalo, New York, at a huge fair for visitors from all over the world, the Pan-American Exposition of 1901.

At the fair Calamity Jane stood along the midway of its amusement section trying to sell her booklets. It was a horrible experience, worse by far than Minneapolis and a million times worse than any hardship she had ever faced under the big sky of the West. How she finally got the money to board a westbound train is not exactly clear — some say that Buffalo Bill himself, for old times' sake, staked her to the price of a ticket back to Deadwood.

By then, Calamity was approaching the age of fifty and having serious health problems. Still she slogged on somehow for another two years, picking up a few dollars every so often by working in a restaurant kitchen. Yet as she kept failing bodily, in another way Old Calam triumphed.

Even the town's most respectable women, as well as their preacher and banker husbands, realized that Calamity Jane had turned into more than a person. She was a part of the great legend that celebrated the freedom and daring of the West in its early days, when it still seemed an unspoiled paradise, without any of the evils of civilization. No matter that legends might not be strictly true; in a larger sense they were truer than any dusty facts — and the legend of the Wild West summed up a marvelous period in American history, just as the legend of King Arthur and his knights summed up the whole era called the Middle Ages.

So when Calamity Jane died in a far from elegant hotel above a saloon — on August 1, 1903, at the age of fifty-one — Deadwood's

Calamity Jane posed for this picture in 1895, hoping it would convince the manager of a Wild West show to hire her. (Adams Memorial Hall Museum, Deadwood)

Deadwood's leading citizens at Calamity Jane's funeral. (*Adams Memorial Hall Museum, Deadwood*)

Old Pioneer Society gave her the most elaborate funeral in the town's history. Mourners crowded a church she had probably never entered during her lifetime, while the Methodist minister delivered a carefully worded sermon stressing her bravery and her generosity.

Then her coffin, covered with flowers, was carried up to the town's hilltop cemetery. Heeding her last wish, they buried her beside the grave of the man she had claimed as her husband, Wild Bill Hickok.

The Legend Lives On

Only two other women played leading roles in the legendary Wild West — the "bandit queen" Belle Starr and the celebrated sharp-shooter Annie Oakley. A few other women acquired lesser fame for other specialties, such as running dance halls.

But the bravery of uncounted wives or daughters who managed to survive all sorts of hardships was mostly ignored because, a hundred years ago, a much higher value was put on the more dramatic activities reserved for men and boys.

Calamity Jane had at least tried to experience the entire range of exciting possibilities that life on the frontier offered. So, gradually, as the twentieth century advanced and old ideas about women's place began to change, a new surge of interest in her arose — stressing her independent spirit and glossing over her failures. "She swore, she drank, she wore men's clothing," one writer put it tolerantly. "She was just ahead of her time."

Then, in the 1930s, newspapers reported a remarkable story. A woman who claimed to be the daughter of Calamity Jane and Wild Bill Hickok had just turned up, carrying a diary that she said Calamity had written over a period of nearly twenty-five years. She offered this as proof of her identity and explained what had happened as follows:

She had been born in a cave near Deadwood, South Dakota, not

49

Belle Starr and her husband. (Denver Public Library, Western History Department)

long after her father had been shot in the Number 10 Saloon. As her mother hovered weakly over her, a kind stranger had peered into the cave. He proved to be the captain of an English ship operated by the prosperous Cunard Line; he was taking time off to feast his eyes on the West's scenic marvels.

Since he and his wife had wished in vain for a child of their own, Captain O'Neil urged the ailing mother to let them adopt her baby. To give her little Janey a better chance in life, Calamity heartbrokenly

Annie Oakley. (Denver Public Library, Western History Department)

Calamity Peak, named after Calamity Jane, near the town of Custer, Montana.
(Library of Congress)

agreed. The captain had taken the baby back across the ocean, where he and his wife had brought her up without telling her of her true parentage.

It was only after the death of her English husband, the woman said, that she had discovered who she really was by reading Calamity Jane's diary, which she had found in an old trunk. Records of the Cunard Line showed no evidence of a captain named O'Neil, and the so-called diary failed to convince any Western history expert of its authenticity, but the woman describing herself as Calamity's daughter was interviewed on Mother's Day by one of the era's most popular radio broadcasters — and a lot of people enjoyed the tale she told.

Although the supposed daughter soon disappeared from public

view, out in Hollywood the idea of using Calamity as a movie heroine took hold. Over the years, a variety of actresses portrayed her, all very differently, depending on the type of entertainment that was most popular at the moment. One film starring the sexy Jane Russell stressed Calamity Jane's love affairs. In another, Jean Arthur was a bashful yet humorous Calam, the pal of strong, silent plainsman Gary Cooper.

Then, during the 1950s, the musical "Calamity Jane," starring perky, blond Doris Day, scored a memorable success. Its Jane was just the sort of likable tomboy who might be living next door in a 1950s ranch house, and its version of her romance with Wild Bill Hickok owed much more to Hollywood song-and-dance talent than to sober historians. Even so, this movie proved to have a lasting appeal — it still turns up now and then on television, and fans often find it on the classics shelf at video-rental shops.

Television has also produced serious as well as fanciful scripts about Calamity Jane. As far away as England, paperback adventure tales with Calamity as their heroine continue to be published. In 1990, the well-known novelist Larry McMurtry made her the heroine of his *Buffalo Girls,* and a young composer named Dora Ohrenstein presented a musical work titled *Calamity Jane to Her Daughter* in a New York theater.

Meanwhile, the West itself has certainly not forgotten her. It is the legend, of course, rather than the real person that attracts tourists to exhibits of doubtful authenticity, like her alleged diary. But the memory of the Calamity herself is cherished, too, especially in Deadwood. A dozen different souvenir postcards offer pictures of her, and stacks of booklets give more or less accurate accounts of her career. "In her own way," as one historian of the West has put it, "she was most certainly somebody."

Sources

Ahearn, Robert G. *The Mythic West in Twentieth Century America.* Lawrence: University of Kansas Press, 1986.

Aikman, Duncan. *Calamity Jane and the Lady Wildcats.* New York: Henry Holt, 1927.

Bennett, Estelline. *Old Deadwood Days.* New York: J. H. Sears, 1928.

Billington, Roy Allen. *America's Frontier Heritage.* New York: Holt, Rinehart and Winston, 1966.

Brown, Edmund. *Dime Novels: Following an Old Trail.* Boston: Little, Brown, 1929.

Cannary, Martha Jane. *Calamity Jane's Letters to Her Daughter.* San Lorenzo, Cal.: Shameless Hussy Press, 1976.

————. *Life and Adventures of Calamity Jane by Herself.* Fairfield, Wash.: Galleon Press, 1969.

Clairmonte, Glenn. *Calamity Was the Name for Jane.* Denver: Sage Books, 1959.

Connell, Evan S. *Son of the Morning Star: Custer and the Little Bighorn.* San Francisco: North Point Press, 1984.

Custer, Elizabeth B. *Boots and Saddle: Life in Dakota with General Custer.* New York: Harper and Brothers, 1885.

DuFran, Dora. *Low Down on Calamity Jane.* Deadwood, S.D.: H.

Rezatto, 1981.

Goetzmann, William H., and William L. Goetzmann. *The West of the Imagination.* New York: W. W. Norton, 1986.

Greever, William S. *The Bonanza West: The Story of Western Mining Rushes, 1848–1900.* Norman: University of Oklahoma Press, 1963.

Griswold, Wesley S. *A Work of Giants: Building the First Transcontinental Railroad.* New York: McGraw Hill, 1962.

Horan, James D. *Desperate Women.* New York: Bonanza, 1962.

Jennewein, J. Leonard. *Calamity Jane of the Western Trails.* Huron, S.D.: Dakota Books, 1953.

Johannsen, Albert. *The House of Beadle and Adams.* 2 vols. Norman: University of Oklahoma Press, 1950.

Klock, Irma M. *Here Comes Calamity Jane.* Deadwood, S.D.: Dakota Graphics, 1979.

Mumey, Nolie. *Calamity Jane: A History of Her Life and Adventures in the West.* Denver: Range Press, 1950.

Parker, Watson. *Gold in the Black Hills.* Norman: University of Oklahoma Press, 1966.

Richardson, Albert D. *Beyond the Mississippi.* Hartford, Conn.: General Publishing Company, 1867.

Schlissel, Lillian. *Women's Diaries of the Western Journey.* New York: Schocken, 1982.

Smith, Henry Nash. *Virgin Land: The American West as Symbol and Myth.* Cambridge, Mass.: Harvard University Press, 1950.

Sollid, Roberta B. *Calamity Jane: A Study in Historical Criticism.* Helena: Historical Society of Montana, 1958.

Turner, Frederick Jackson. *The Frontier in American History.* New York: Holt, Rinehart and Winston, 1947.

Suggested Further Readings
for Young Readers

Alderman, Clifford L. *Annie Oakley.* New York: Macmillan, 1979.

Alter, Judith. *Growing Up in the Old West.* New York: Franklin Watts, 1989.

Bailey, Ralph Edgar. *Wagons Westward! The Story of Alexander Majors.* New York: William Morrow, 1969.

Collier, Edmund. *The Story of Buffalo Bill.* New York: Grosset & Dunlap, 1952.

Freedman, Russell. *Children of the Wild West.* New York: Ticknor & Fields, 1983.

————. *Cowboys of the Wild West.* New York: Ticknor & Fields, 1985.

Goble, Paul, and Dorothy Goble. *Red Hawk's Account of Custer's Last Stand.* New York: Pantheon, 1969.

Moody, Ralph. *Kit Carson and the Wild Frontier.* New York: Random House, 1955.

Stewart, George. *The Pioneers Go West.* New York: Random House, 1954.

Surge, Frank. *Western Outlaws.* Minneapolis: Lerner Publications, 1970.

Acknowledgments

In writing this book and assembling its illustrations, I have received much generous help at many libraries and picture archives. But before listing at least some of those to whom I am most indebted, I must thank my good friend and fellow author Leslie Wheeler and her husband, Bob Stein, who, during a summer visit to her family's home in Montana, served invaluably as my research aides at the Montana Historical Society's headquarters in Helena and also at various archives in South Dakota — even bringing me back a Calamity Jane T-shirt from some souvenir shop along their travels.

Meanwhile, Mary Lou Alm at the Pine Plains Library near my home in New York's Hudson Valley, with unfailing patience, secured dozens of books for me through the wonderful facilities of the national interlibrary loan system. Several staff members at Vassar College's fine library also assisted me in my quest for Western lore.

Among all the others who provided helpful guidance or useful material, such as sheafs of photocopied clippings from old newspapers, I want to mention Professor James McLaird of the History Department at Dakota Wesleyan University; Eleanor M. Gehres, manager of the Denver Public Library's Western History Department, and Kathey Swan and Philip Panum on her staff; Terri Davis, director of the

Deadwood Public Library; Ann B. Jenks of the South Dakota Historical Society; Jane Kolbe, state librarian at the South Dakota State Library; and Anne Marie Baker, curator of Adams Memorial Hall Museum in Deadwood.

In connection with my assembling of pictures, I am most grateful to numerous staff members at the National Archives and Records Administration, at the Prints and Photos Division and the Photo-duplication Service of the Library of Congress, and at several of the archives branches of the Smithsonian Institution in Washington.

Index